# DON'T LEAVE IT
# TO THE DOGS

By:
Michael Ray Van

AiON MULTIMEDIA
Is 40:8

Coverstock Photography by Kajano

Printed in the United States of America
ISBN# 978-0-9852986-9-2

Published by Aion Multimedia
20118 N 67th Ave
Suite 300-446
Glendale AZ 85308
www.aionmultimedia.com

# TABLE OF CONTENTS

# Chapter 1:
# OUT OF DARKNESS

What are some of your first memories? **I** remember things like going to preschool and having to paste paper together for different school projects in order to decorate the school room or take home to my parents. Oh yeah, **I** enjoyed the taste of the paste. Didn't you? **I** was from a sports family that excelled in all sports. **I** had great friends and we would talk about what we would do or be when we grew up. **I** remember in elementary school, we were given ledger cards showing many types of career possibilities and the assignment was to choose two or three future careers of your interest. One of my career choices was to be an oceanographer because we used to go swimming a lot during summer vacation. **I** also liked drawing racing cars. I wanted to go to college, wanted to be a movie star or recording artist, enjoyed the company of women, wanted to play football, baseball, boxing, etc.

You are probably thinking the **(I)'s** have it. Well, you are right! A lot of the thoughts, dreams and memories were pursued and accomplished with good and bad results! All my life was filled with momentary success stories that included an area of darkness. I really thought I had everything under control, but often found myself in unwanted places, such as in jail, then probation, and even prison. Some of you know what I'm talking about, when I say, I was one of those guys that said to himself, "I don't belong in this place!" But found myself addicted to drugs and repeating the same insanity of using over and over again. Of course, I had some periods of sanity while under the supervision of the legal system (having to go to court, probation, jail, prison etc.). In those times, I would put some concentration on reading the Bible and started taking some of the right steps (going to AA, Anger Management classes, and taking college courses) by leading what I thought was a good life. However, sooner or later my focus would become warped because of my fleshly interest for women, drugs, and money.

Coming out of the darkness was and is truly by the grace of God. Somehow, during my drug addiction, I found myself holding on to the Bible with one hand and with the other hand, I was holding onto a glass pipe smoking crack. I used to stay up days and nights reading the word of the Lord. When I took a drag or puff of the pipe, I was immediately driven to read Bible verses out loud. My fear drove me to read during my affliction. During this smoking/reading marathon, my thoughts would wrestle with things I used to partake in such as pornography, being with women, drinking, carousing, etc., but I never would get the complete satisfaction of doing what came to mind. This went on for years. Then there was a brief period where the smoking ceased and I found myself only concentrating on God's word and my life was changing. I felt like my addiction was all over, but from time to time, I wanted to enact some of the same old experiences. Guess what? It happened again! Next door to me was a woman that my mind envisioned as being the type of lady, physically, that I would like be with. It was too perfect of a picture, because I was married! I'm sure you know my mind wasn't hearing that! So backwards, I went to an adulterous relationship with her and then back to drugs.

Eventually, I found myself back in a room with a crack pipe in one hand and the Bible in the other. I know, it's strange to me too! This went on for many more years and my mind had convinced me that maybe this is what I was supposed to do in order to keep me from my lust. Let's face it, my mind was muddled. I was interpreting scripture incorrectly. Such as:

> *1 Timothy 4:16 (KJV)*
> *"Take heed unto yourself, and unto the doctrine; continue in them: for in doing this you shall both save yourself, and them that hear you."*

I used the word of God incorrectly; I used it to justify my condition and to continue on in it. I know now that I didn't hear the whole first half of the scripture, "Take heed unto yourself, and unto the doctrine." Anyway, my way of life began to take its toll on my body. As the years proceeded, fatigue began to settle in during these marathon readings, but God's unwarranted grace continued for me, and I was able to complete what I thought had to be done during each reading session. Then, one day after five days of reading the word of God, I decided to go for a walk in order to get some air into my brain. During this walk there was a woman across the street. I noticed she was paying some attention to me and my focus on God left me. Once again, lust had taken root. To make a long story short, because of my inability to keep my focus, I found myself being dragged down into the same deep pit, which I had seen years ago. Same street drag, same prostitutes, and same street game. The woman I saw during this encounter was also a drug addict. She was more interested in looking for more drugs, but my concentration was bent on sex. Neither was accomplished during this long drawn out day and now I had to face myself. In my delusion, I felt it had been a while since I had actually gone this far in losing complete concentration. I was doing everything I could to

3

fulfill my quest for lust, which was something I wasn't accustomed to doing during this bizarre ritual of reading my Bible and smoking crack.

So after this long drawn out day, I finally returned home to my wife. I struggled to close my eyes in order to get some rest, but a deep and fearful guilt came over me. I was afraid in ways that I can't even describe. I conceived the pit of Hell. Then, I felt alone and an eerie detachment from God that was worse than the thought of going to Hell. The only words I could manage to say at that time were **Jesus is the Lord, Jesus is the Lord, and Jesus is the Lord!**

Then, when I called on the name of **Jesus** I began to seek Him with a determined heart. I realized that I no longer wanted to play this game with our **Father**. I never wanted to feel lost again. I felt a need to have a true relationship, talk with Him every day, learn His love and love Him in return by being obedient. Now, I call Him **ABBA/Father**. I stay connected to him with a **God kind of faith**. The following chapters will give you information on how God is working through faith in my life. God's hand is revealed through my Spiritual Father Pastor (Apostle) Gene Herndon, in addition to his Fathers in the faith, Reverend Ricky Edwards, Dr. Ed Dufresne, "Dad" Kenneth E. Hagin and the many others that God has blessed in his ministry.

Truly this was how I was, this is how I am now and Jesus made all the difference. Walking in Jesus, who is my God given faith, He is everything that I was looking for and on the cross He was given to me a long time ago. A loving Father, His Son Jesus Christ, and the living Holy Spirit, a beautiful wife (Lori Van), my son, grandkids and all those of the body of Christ. Every day is filled with His love and His faith.

# Chapter 2:
# FAITH BEGINS WHERE THE WILL OF GOD IS KNOWN

My spiritual grandfather, Reverend Ricky Edwards says in his book, "Phases and Rooms" that Christianity is based upon faith. If you explained to somebody the life of Jesus, it would take faith to believe that He (Jesus) was born from a woman who had never been with a man. It would take faith to know that Jesus walked the Earth for 30 years, then healed many. He was then crucified and descended into Hell. Not only that, but He rose on the third day and picked up His body to show to many people for forty days. He left on a cloud while angels proclaimed He would come back the same way. You can't prove that to anybody. What we see in the word of God, is a faith based belief. There are people who have tried to prove that the word of God is just another book. To those that do not have the spirit of God, or refuse to believe in it, it's just another autobiography or history book. To those who do believe, it's God speaking to them. It's a faith-based belief.

In Chapter 1, Out of Darkness, I spoke of my afflictions and the reaction(s) they caused in my life. You can see my thought process was misguided. I was walking in faith, but faithful to the things of this world. I was faithful to things that were seen, heard, tasted, smelled, and touched. My mind never fully comprehended that Satan, the god of this world, was there to capitalize on my mistakes. Satan is subtle. If you have not been saved or have been saved and are **unskilled in God's Word**, Satan will have your life in contention (discord). He is always looking for a Christian who has strayed away from the pack (the body of Christ).

The Word of God says:

*1 Peter 5:8(KJV)*
***"Be sober, be vigilant; because your adversary the devil, as a roaring lion, walketh about, seeking whom he may devour."***

My Spiritual Father and Pastor, Apostle Gene Herndon gives a visualization of this scripture. Picture a Lion in Africa, out in the jungle and on a quest for food. When the lion sees its prey, (which mainly consists of large mammals such as Antelopes, Gazelles, Warthogs, Wildebeest, Buffalos and Zebras), the Lion will creep up on the prey, when he gets close enough, he will let out a roar that confuses the animal(s). The Lion doesn't go into the crowd of animals, but will go after the weak. The weak prey has gone astray and doesn't run with the pack.

Just like the Lion, Satan capitalizes on our mistakes. Satan seeks people who are alone and have gone astray, including the, "it's just me and JC (Jesus Christ)" crowd. The "JC and me" crowd are those who feel that it is not important to have a Pastor and do not attend church.

Our Father says in:

*Hebrews 13:7 (KJV)*

*"Remember your leaders, those who spoke to you the word of God. Consider the outcome of their way of life, and imitate their faith".*

You can see in Hebrews 13:7, it says to remember your leaders, those who spoke to you the word of God... The way God has spoken to the men of God in my life has allowed me to benefit from their evaluated experiences. The only way that I'm able to benefit from this word is to listen to what is said and apply it to my life. In fact, there is no way of completely understanding the word that is spoken unless we take the first step and do what the word says. Let's take something like playing catch with a coach. The coach explains to us how to catch the ball because he has experienced catching a ball. He has given us the knowledge on how to accomplish catching the ball, right? But we still haven't caught the ball yet. Okay now, he prepares himself to throw the ball in order for it to be caught by us. By his faith, not ours, because we have never caught the ball before, we have positioned ourselves to catch the ball. We have put our trust in him to deliver the ball in a way that would enable us to catch it.

In a similar fashion, God has given us leaders who have become skillful in spiritual knowledge that will only benefit you. Watch and consider the outcome of their way of life, and imitate their faith.

He also says in:

**Hebrews 10:25** *(KJV)*
*"Not forsaking the assembling of ourselves together, as the manner of some is; but exhorting one another: and so much the more, as ye see the day approaching."*

7

Looking faithfully into Hebrews 10:25, you notice after it says, "Not forsaking the assembling of ourselves," it adds "but exhorting one another." *Exhorting* is to strongly encourage someone. Here, they are mentioning encouraging one another to faith, love, and good works. We have a direct relationship and responsibility to one another. This relationship is in the body of Christ.

*1 Corinthians 12: 12-26 (KJV)*
*"For as the body is one, and hath many members, and all the members of that one body, being many, are one body: so also is Christ. For by one Spirit are we all baptized into one body, whether we be Jews or Gentiles, whether we be bond or free; and have been all made to drink into one Spirit. For the body is not one member, but many. If the foot shall say, Because I am not the hand, I am not of the body; is it therefore not of the body? And if the ear shall say, Because I am not the eye, I am not of the body; is it therefore not of the body? If the whole body were an eye, where were the hearing? If the whole were hearing, where were the smelling? But now hath God set the members very one of them in the body, as it hath pleased him. And if they were all one member, where were the body? But now are they many members, yet but one body. And the eye cannot say unto the hand, I have no need of thee: nor again the head to the feet, I have no need of you. Nay, much more those members of the body, which seem to be more feeble, are necessary: And those members of the body, which we think to be less honourable, upon these we bestow more abundant*

*honour; and our uncomely parts have more abundant comeliness. For our comely parts have no need: but God hath tempered the body together, having given more abundant honour to that part which lacked: That there should be no schism in the body; but that the members should have the same care one for another. And whether one member suffer, all the members suffer with it; or one member be honoured, all the members rejoice with it."*

Recognizing our faith portion in the body of Christ is essential. The body can only function by listening to the Head. Have you ever seen a body that was just an eye or a body that was only an ear? Besides not being able to sustain life, it would be a little strange and we could never get the complete sense of life's experiences. The body has different functions that work together as one. It's the same with the body of Christ. When we live faithfully to Christ within His body, we are able to be taught the truth of scripture, trained for service, and helped to mature spiritually, being used in His purpose to go out into the world.

I've learned and continue to learn that I must be immovable to Gods word. I must forget about those things learned in my past and not lean to my own understanding. I want to steer clear of, "Me Faith,"and instead I will hold on to every Word and Revelation given to me by the Holy Ghost. Knowing, Satan is waiting for his opportunity to pounce. I must do as it states in 1 Peter:

*1 Peter 5:8-10 (AMP)*
*"Be well balanced (temperate, sober of mind), be vigilant and cautious at all times; for that enemy of yours, the devil, roams around like a lion roaring [in*

9

*fierce hunger], seeking someone to seize upon and devour. Withstand him; be firm in faith [against his onset--rooted, established, strong, immovable, and determined], knowing that the same (identical) sufferings are appointed to your brotherhood (the whole body of Christians) throughout the world. And after you have suffered a little while, the God of all grace [Who imparts all blessing and favor], Who has called you to His [own] eternal glory in Christ Jesus, will Himself complete and make you what you ought to be, establish and ground you securely, and strengthen, and settle you."*

It's really important to take to heart 1 Peter 5:8, knowing that we must be well balanced in the word of God, and then vigilant; being cautious at all times. In order to be well balanced in God's word, we must have a steady diet of His word implanted within our heart. Without God's word on any given subject, there is no way to know if we have been, if we are currently being, or if we are going to be deceived. We have to come to the realization that Satan has been here a long time and he is waiting for those who are unclear in God's Spirit of Truth. For instance, if we accept what we've learned in this world, such as a cold, your doctor will say you have a cold or an associate will hear you cough and ask you, "Do you have a cold?" Jesus said in:

*1 Peter 2:24 (KJV)*
*"Who his own self bare our sins in his own body on the tree, that we, being dead to sins, should live unto righteousness: by whose stripes ye were healed."*

Which word bares more clout? The doctors, the associates question, or the words spoken by Jesus? If we are living by this world's way of thinking- by sight, hearing, smell, taste, and touch,- we might agree with the doctor or the associate's question. But, we have a choice to choose the words of Christ and be strong, immovable, and determined to His will. By choosing His will you are accepting your authority over the god of this world and operating in God's spiritual body of being healed.

To give you a better understanding of this, let's take a portion from the book, "identity: Discovering Your Authority in Christ," written by my Spiritual Father, Apostle Gene Herndon.

"Why won't the gates of hell prevail against it? Jesus continued and said, 'I will give you the keys.' So the gates of hell will not prevail against you because Jesus has given you the key to it! Jesus continued by saying Satan will not prevail against you because you have the key. Let me tell you what the key is. Whatever you bind on earth shall be bound in heaven. Whatever you loose on earth shall be loosed in heaven. In other words, what you permit him to do; he has every right to continue. You might passively sit there asking Satan to stop bothering your family, but it is not until you push back that he responds. Remember the woman who came to the feet of Jesus and asked for healing for her daughter and Jesus replied, 'This is not for the dogs,' She said, 'Yes, but even the dogs get a crumb.' As a Christian, you must realize that you have authority over your child. So 'Satan,' you can demand, 'take your hands off my child. I'm not asking you, I'm telling you in the name of Jesus! This is not a discussion, do it right now!'"

Knowing God's will is the key to prayer, spiritual growth and fruitfulness in our individual lives. So by our obedience to Christ and being confident to His will, we are able to use these tools, right now, in this world. When you use these tools, you realize the power of God's love. His love is given to you by your faith. His faith is His will! The more faith we yield to in our life, the more we become like Christ. Living in faith makes us Christ like and therefore Christians.

This concept eluded me for some years. I believed in Jesus and was baptized at 13-years old, but I never walked according to the Word of God. As you read earlier, living each day unto myself, I never knew how to completely live unto God and there was never a conviction to follow Him totally. "Just enough" was sufficient. I never realized that this mentality was taking me in harm's way and keeping me from living in perfect peace.

Apostle Gene Herndon explains the importance of being confident to Christ's will:

> Completes us
> Makes you what you ought to be
> Establishes us
> Grounds you securely
> Strengthens you
> Settles us

Recognizing that whatever I go through, "It is what it is until God tells me." We must be patient and wait for God. Remembering the abundance of the heart is what you will speak. So when you position yourself with those God has set over you (such as a pastor), it will enhance your thought life.

**Philippians 4:6-8 (CEB)**
*"Don't be anxious about anything; rather, bring up all of your requests to God in your prayers and petitions, along with giving thanks. Then the peace of God that exceeds all understanding will keep your hearts and minds safe in Christ Jesus. From now on, brothers*

**and sisters, if anything is excellent and if anything is admirable, focus your thoughts on these things: all that is true, all that is holy, all that is just, all that is pure, all that is lovely, and all that is worthy of praise."**

> We have to be disciplined
> In control of our mouths
> Clearly make our requests known
> Thank God for all things

When we give thanks, we are receiving what has already been given to us. It doesn't matter what your situation seems to look like, you have to remember that God said it, you believe it, and that settles it. Faith is what we do!

The Merriam-Webster definition for *Faith*:
A. allegiance to duty or a person: loyalty
B. fidelity to one's promises: sincerity of intentions
C. belief and trust in and loyalty to God: belief in the traditional doctrines of a religion
D. firm belief in something for which there is no proof: complete trust
E. something that is believed especially with strong conviction; especially: a system of  religious beliefs <the Protestant *faith*> **on faith :** Without question

So, I continue by using God's word to guide me. Believing and trusting Him without question, being loyal to Him, with confidence in His promises, and realizing my responsibilities to

Him. Thanking Him for keeping me prosperous, healthy, whole and wise.

Paul said, "I fight the good fight of faith."

> **2 Timothy 4:7 *(KJV)***
> *"I have fought a good fight, I have finished my course, I have kept the faith."*

This tells me that faith is what we rely on. That's it! I keep my eyes upon God, casting all of my care upon him. Knowing God's thoughts are higher than my thoughts. If it is not the word of God, it doesn't exist. Everything is revealed by God.

> **1 *Peter* 5: 7-8 *(AMP)***
> *"Casting the whole of your care [all your anxieties, all your worries, all your concerns, once and for all] on Him, for He cares for you affectionately and cares about you watchfully. Be well balanced (temperate, sober of mind), be vigilant and cautious at all times; for that enemy of yours, the devil, roams around like a lion roaring [in fierce hunger], seeking someone to seize upon and devour."*

Faith is a knowing on the inside of you. God truly is a respecter of a God type of faith. When you know God's will and God's will is His Word, His Word will empower you to prosper.

The Merriam-Webster definition for Prosper:

> **A.** to succeed in an enterprise or activity; *especially* : to achieve economic success
> B. to become strong and flourishing

So, with this understanding we can look at God's word *in Isaiah 55:11-12.*

**Isaiah 55:11-12 (KJV)**
**"So shall my word be that goeth forth out of my mouth: it shall not return unto me void, but it shall accomplish that which I please, and it shall prosper in the thing whereto I sent it. For ye shall go out with joy, and be led forth with peace: the mountains and the hills shall break forth before you into singing, and all the trees of the field shall clap their hands."**

We have been given a promise by God that although we were great in our sins, we have been released from our bondage and can live in peace with joy in our hearts. So God gave the word in Isaiah, I have faith in that word and because I have complete trust in this word it produces for me (Safety and Joy).

Loyalty to God's word gives you an authority in which you can command Satan to take his hands off of your finances, relationships and dispatch angels and guardians on God's behalf in any situation. In Jesus name. Amen.

If you know God's will, remain disciplined, trust Him,and then your soul will prosper. That means everything you touch will prosper. God wants your soul (mind, will, and emotions) to prosper, to be an abundant supply for His glory, and have more than enough in order to lead others to Christ. This all starts by knowing the will of God and seeking Him first.

**Matthew 6:33 (KJV)**

*"But seek ye first the kingdom of God, and his righteousness; and all these things shall be added unto you."*

When we truly seek God, seeking Him only, He begins to reign in our heart. His faith becomes a part of us and we can stand on God's good soil without being wishy washy. The word of God gives us an illustration of this in Mark 4:14-20.

*Mark 4:14-20 (KJV)*
*"The sower soweth the word. And these are they by the way side, where the word is sown; but when they have heard, Satan cometh immediately, and taketh away the word that was sown in their hearts. And these are they likewise which are sown on stony ground; who, when they have heard the word, immediately receive it with gladness; And have no root in themselves, and so endure but for a time: afterward, when affliction or persecution ariseth for the word's sake, immediately they are offended. And these are they which are sown among thorns; such as hear the word, And the cares of this world, and the deceitfulness of riches, and the lusts of other things entering in, choke the word, and it becometh unfruitful. And these are they which are sown on good ground; such as hear the word, and receive it, and bring forth fruit, some thirtyfold, some sixty, and some an hundred."*

Notice the ones which produced heard the word, and received it, and then it brought forth fruit; some thirtyfold, some sixty, and some a hundred. They were walking by faith and led by the Holy Spirit. We have to realize that Satan is temporal and God is eternal. We have to maintain God's patience, stay in His will, wait for Him and remain in His peace.

>*Isaiah 26:3 (KJV)*
>*"Thou wilt keep him in perfect peace, whose mind is stayed on thee: because he trusteth in thee."*

# Chapter 3:
# GOD KIND OF FAITH

Many of us have a job, wife, car, house, money, bicycle, family, girlfriend or boyfriend. If we aren't feeling up to those things, we have ourselves. We often apply a lot of faith to those things around us. When something happens to disrupt that relationship, we feel like our faith has let us down. We've learned to trust in the things we see.

When I was kid, I enjoyed watching Star Trek and other science fiction movies. In one Star Trek episode called, "The Apple", the crew of the Enterprise visits a planet that they thought resembled paradise. The planet in its appearance was tropical and it had high quantities of resources. They soon found out that the planet was drastically hostile. The planet had explosive rocks and bizarre lightning storms. Captain Kirk started to lose team members of his away team. An energy field on the planet interfered with the ships transporters. So Captain Kirk was not able to transport any of his team members back to the ship. The Enterprise crew went to a primitive village to avoid the planet's hazards. In this village was a group of people who were assigned to be, "Keepers of Vaal". "Vaal" was a rock formation that had a dragon-like head figure on one side. Spock, concluded that there was a computer system underground. Vaal in the story was a god type of figure, with a supply of explosive rocks from the planet and energy resources for food and shelter. Vaal was a computer system that kept this society from procreating. In this science fiction story these villagers submitted totally, with trust and conviction to a computer machine! They were young and healthy, but lacking in knowledge. They lived submitted to a lie. They were totally unaware. Just like the TV episode, many of us are submitted to the ways of this world. We live in the lie and we are totally unaware. We have to realize the ways of the world are not of God. The world's way is the accuser of our brethren. He has many names: Devil, Dragon, [False] Angel of Light, god of This World, Father of Lies, Lucifer, Murderer, Prince of The Power of The Air, Satan, Serpent, Son of The Morning, and The Spirit of Antichrist.

As a Christian, we must always be sure of victory of God's power and faithfulness to His people, us!

> *Psalm 20:6-7 (KJV)*
> *"Now know I that the LORD saveth his anointed; he will hear him from his holy heaven with the saving strength of his right hand. Some trust in chariots, and some in horses: but we will remember the name of the LORD our God."*

Psalm 20:6 tells us to have complete trust in our Lord. That we know that the Lord saveth his anointed, in the saving strength of His right hand!

Do you know the Lord and do you have complete trust in Him? Have you really asked yourself, "Do I really believe in Christ?" The answer should be "yes." I believe Christ is part of God the Father, who you and I have never seen. He was sent as God's only Son, who we also have never seen. He was born from a virgin, He lived here on this earth for approximately 33 years. Jesus Christ walked with and taught His disciples. He was beaten beyond recognition, suffered for us and died for us. Jesus descended into hell, then He ascended up on high. He set the captive free and gave gifts unto men.

It takes faith to believe all of this! Okay, if we believe that, we can conclude Jesus is more than the perfect example of faith. He is faith. He is the God kind of faith. God's gift to us!

*Ephesians 4:4-16 (KJV)*
*"There is one body, and one Spirit, even as ye are called in one hope of your calling; One Lord, one faith, one baptism, One God and Father of all, who is above all, and through all, and in you all. But unto every one of us is given grace according to the measure of the gift of Christ. Wherefore he saith, When he ascended up on high, he led captivity captive, and gave gifts unto men. (Now that he ascended, what is it but that he also descended first into the lower parts of the earth? He that descended is the same also that ascended up far above all heavens, that he might fill all things. And he gave some, apostles; and some, prophets; and some, evangelists; and some, pastors and teachers; For the perfecting of the saints, for the work of the ministry, for the edifying of the body of Christ: Till we all come in the unity of the faith, and of the knowledge of the Son of God, unto a perfect man, unto the measure of the stature of the fulness of Christ: That we henceforth be no more children, tossed to and fro, and carried about with every wind of doctrine, by the sleight of men, and cunning craftiness, whereby they lie in wait to*

*deceive; But speaking the truth in love, may grow up into him in all things, which is the head, even Christ: From whom the whole body fitly joined together and compacted by that which every joint supplieth, according to the effectual working in the measure of every part, maketh increase of the body unto the edifying of itself in love."*

The word in Ephesians 4:4-16 says there is one Lord, one faith, one baptism, one God and Father of all. God is above all, and through all, and in us all. He gives unto every one of us grace according to the measure of the gift of Christ.

Christ has given us the gift of the Holy Spirit, which is the full measure, unto ALL men. In Ephesians it is telling us the gift has already been given! The word also says, "He gave some to be apostles; and some, prophets; and some, evangelists; and some, pastors and teachers; for the perfecting of the saints." This is for the work of the ministry and to edify of the body of Christ.

Suppose someone decides to give you a 55' inch LCD TV and it is still in the box. You didn't ask for it. They gave it to you as a gift. You take it home and now you want to watch it, but you've never set up a TV before! You can't just open up the box and plug it in. Well, you can, but most of the time that will not work. So, you have to look at the manual on how to set up the TV and the remote. You have to read about the safety instructions, and others things.

The manual is written in English, but to you it looks like Chinese. You attempt to read the instructions line by line, you sit on the floor with a pencil in your mouth and start reading out loud. It says in the instructions to connect the LCD TV to a cable box or satellite receiver using an HDMI cable. You continue to read, the ends of the HDMI cable is flat, and one end should plug into the "HDMI In" slot on the back of the television. The other end goes in the "HDMI" slot on the back of the cable box or satellite receiver. Step two: Turn on the cable box or satellite receiver and television. Step three: With the remote control, press the "Menu" button to access television features and settings. Step four: In the menu, press the up and down arrows and select "Channel" on the screen. You continue to read the instruction manual.

You think to yourself, "Whew, no problem I can do that." You complete everything as you thought the manual read. You turn on the TV and guess what? It is not working! So, you look at the pictures in the manual to get a visual perspective. You double check and you still think everything is setup right. The TV still doesn't work! It's time to call someone who knows how to setup a TV. Someone you have faith in to help you accomplish your goal. The bottom line is the gift was given and now learning how to use the gift is important.

We have been given a gift from God; Jesus Christ and Him Crucified. We have also been given apostles; prophets; evangelists; pastors and teachers. All to perfect us as saints. They are training us for the work of the ministry. They are helping to edify the body of Christ. Edify means to instruct and improve especially in moral and religious knowledge. The only way to instruct someone and build them up in the body of Christ is to use the word of God. The word of God is God's will for our life. When we operate in His will, the results are a God kind of faith. In order to attain faith in anything, we must first hear the word. Think about that for a moment, when have you ever had faith in anything without first having been informed of it?

*Romans 10:17 (KJV)*
*"So then faith cometh by hearing, and hearing by the*
*word of God."*

We can have faith in anything by hearing it. The word goes on to say, "And hearing by the word of God." We have a manual, a living blue print given to us by God. In the Holy Bible there are 7,000 promises. That's 7,000 ways to increase our faith and to live as God wills us to live. There are 7,000 promises to hear and 7,000 promises to memorize and apply to your life. There are 7,000 promises to meditate on and 7,000 promises to keep us skilled. That's 7,000 promises He wants us to have! That's 7,000 promises that show us He cares, and 7,000 promises that show us His will!

*1 John 5:14 -15 (KJV)*
*"And this is the confidence that we have in him, that,*
*if we ask any thing according to his will, he heareth*
*us: And if we know that he hear us, whatsoever we*
*ask, we know that we have the petitions that we*
*desired of him."*

Once we know what His will is, then we know what to pray for. We are no longer hoping when we pray. We are in agreement with what our Father wants for us! His love is in us! When we pray we can have complete confidence that our Father hears us. Why? God has a plan for us and God desires His plan to be fulfilled in our lives. His plan comes through our obedience.

*Mark 11:22-24 (AMP)*
*"And Jesus, replying, said to them, Have faith in God*
*[constantly]. Truly I tell you, whoever says to this*
*mountain, Be lifted up and thrown into the sea! and*

***does not doubt at all in his heart but believes that what he says will take place, it will be done for him."***

In Mark 11, Jesus said, "Have the faith of God." A God kind of faith at all times. When we have the mind of Christ we are praying in alignment with the will of God. When we know God's will, the stuff that Satan attempts to deceive us will no longer work in our life. Greed, envy, selfishness, and other things of this world are overcome.

We have to believe what God says in this scripture! Truly believe what He says. We have to hold on to His word and act on the word. Jesus has already told us to believe according to the scriptures and to pray and believe. We have to believe even when we don't see the answer. Just believe and it will be done.

# Chapter 4:
# GUARDING YOUR HEART

When you walk in the faith of God you begin to notice two worlds co-existing. There is the seen world (the things we see) and the unseen world (the things we do not see). The seen world has an apparent reality. It is the world we know through our minds and our five senses. The second world is only given to us by Godly revelation. There is a greater percent of people whose lives are focused on the seen world, than those who have come to know God's truth. This means most people live according to their minds and their five senses. They are affected by the things they see, hear, taste, smell, and touch. Their emotions are being driven by their senses.

We've all experienced the first world. We want to watch the latest movie or want to know the latest news. We tell someone our need for money or we feel the need for companionship. We want to taste this or that and we want to feel good. We have to tell someone how we're feeling during our day. We want a wife or husband. We want to let someone know if we're catching a cold, tired or sleepy. We tell someone if we need a drink, a buzz, or a cigarette. We complain if someone hurts us, we have to pay a bill or someone dies. The list goes on and on and on!

If you think about it, our seen world resembles the movie "The Matrix." In this movie, most of the Earth's society was oblivious to how they were living. Their minds were being controlled by the computer imageries that were so real. They were unaware that it was just a computer putting the image in their mind and they were not really living that life. In this movie, the people could see, hear, taste, smell, and touch everything in that computerized world! As infants, they were raised by a computer world and they knew no other world.

If we are not careful we can find ourself standing with one foot in both worlds and never attaining the love God has for us. We have to utilize the word of God to keep His love implanted within our heart.

Proverbs 4:20-27 is where King David (A Man After God's Own Heart) was talking to his son. When reading this scripture, I hear God speaking directly to me. He has me on His knee, and in a comforting tone He says:

**Proverbs 4:20-27 (KJV)**
*"My son, attend to my words; incline thine ear unto my sayings. Let them not depart from thine eyes; keep them in the midst of thine heart. For they are life unto those that find them, and health to all their flesh. Keep thy heart with all diligence; for out of it are the issues of life. Put away from thee a froward mouth, and perverse lips put far from thee. Let thine eyes look right on, and let thine eyelids look straight before thee. Ponder the path of thy feet, and let all thy ways be established. Turn not to the right hand nor to the left: remove thy foot from evil."*

Notice in Proverbs 4:20-21, the word cautions us saying, to attend to "my words", incline thine ear unto my sayings, let them not depart from thine eyes, and doing this in order to keep them in the midst of thine heart. This implies that we must take action by paying special attention to His words. We must do more than just hear His words. We must also follow His words closely. We must do what His word says and submit. He says all those who keep these instructions find life and all health in their flesh. This is a warning from God to keep our heart with all diligence (being consistent) in order to keep us clear of the dangers that can come against us! This is important! The word *heart* is used many times in the Bible. Most of the time the word HEART is used to represent the inner man: our spirit. However, many times it also refers to our mind, will, and emotions also known as the soul. He doesn't want your heart to be corrupted by the seen world or by the god of this world. We have to be diligent in keeping our heart, so that we remain in the life of God and remain healthy. We all should crave to be like David, a man after God's heart. When we live with our confidence in Christ, we are living a full life. We live full in everything and in any situation. We are no longer serving out of obligation, but in admiration and joy for Him.

I remember in the movie "Forrest Gump", Forrest, the main character says, "Momma said, 'Life is like a box of chocolates, you never know what you're going to get.'" Well, that's absolutely wrong! If you know Jesus, there is no mystery! God wants to keep us in the knowing. Jesus said I am the way, and the truth and the life. He also said in:

**John 14:27 (KJV)**
*"Peace I leave with you; my peace I give you. I do not give to you as the world gives. Do not let your hearts be troubled and do not be afraid."*

He didn't say, "I leave peace on earth." He said, "I leave peace with you, my peace!" He gives His peace to be within us, to guard us from any weapon formed against us. You should hear God's love in these words. Child of God--He cares for you! Your Godly revelation in every situation should be that you know, that you know, that you know, that He will never leave you. He will never forsake you. If we are diligent to His truth, He will garrison our hearts. We don't go by what we feel. We only go by what we know. We know this because of the resurrection of Christ.

> *1 Peter 1:3-5 (AMP)*
> *"Praised (honored, blessed) be the God and Father of our Lord Jesus Christ (the Messiah)! By His boundless mercy we have been born again to an everliving hope through the resurrection of Jesus Christ from the dead, [Born anew] into an inheritance which is beyond the reach of change and decay [imperishable], unsullied and unfading, reserved in heaven for you, Who are being guarded (garrisoned) by God's power through [your] faith [till you fully inherit that final] salvation that is ready to be revealed [for you] in the last time."*

The word here says, "Blessed be God and Father of our Lord Jesus Christ." This is Jesus' Father, with respect to His divine nature and His God, with respect to His human part. He has begotten us again unto a lively hope. Christ the living hope. Everything we now have in the faith of Christ is beyond reach of the seen world, the god of this world. Until the end comes we are guarded by God's power through our faith.

> *1 Peter 1:5 (KJV)*

*"Who are kept by the power of God through faith unto salvation ready to be revealed in the last time."*

We are kept! The inheritance is reserved and we, as the heirs, are kept for it. This is the power of God which works in us all. This guards us against all our enemies. Through faith alone our salvation is both received and retained. God cares for us because of the living hope in us. God makes every day better than the last when we continue to be attentive to His word and cast away our cares unto Him.

> *1 Peter 5:4-7 (AMP)*
> *"And [then] when the Chief Shepherd is revealed, you will win the conqueror's crown of glory. Likewise, you who are younger and of lesser rank, be subject to the elders (the ministers and spiritual guides of the church)--[giving them due respect and yielding to their counsel]. Clothe (apron) yourselves, all of you, with humility [as the garb of a servant, so that its covering cannot possibly be stripped from you, with freedom from pride and arrogance] toward one another. For God sets Himself against the proud (the insolent, the overbearing, the disdainful, the presumptuous, the boastful)--[and He opposes, frustrates, and defeats them], but gives grace (favor, blessing) to the humble. Therefore humble yourselves [demote, lower yourselves in your own estimation] under the mighty hand of God, that in due time He may exalt you, Casting the whole of your care [all your anxieties, all your worries, all your concerns, once and for all] on Him, for He cares for you affectionately and cares about you watchfully."*

We have a Chief Shepherd, and His name is Jesus Christ. He has crowned us with glory. He tells us, as the sheep, we are to be subject to our ministers and spiritual leaders of the church. God has appointed shepherds under Christ to lead His sheep. We must give our shepherds respect and yield to their sound counsel. According to the word, we are also to clothe ourselves with humility. We are to be a servant not serving in pride or arrogance. By being a servant we will never be stripped. By being obedient to God's word, we recognize God in those who are over us in the Lord. In submission, we too hear the Gift (The Holy Spirit) of God speaking directly to us through the man or woman of God. Our Father also says that we are to humble ourselves under His mighty hand in all trouble, that He may exalt us in due time. There is a reward for our obedience.

Cast ALL of your cares on Him. Your cares include all your anxieties, worries, concerns and plans. We tend to forget about CASTING all of our cares on Him and will cast only part of our cares upon Him. We might cast one or two cares on Him and forget about the others. We hold on to our other cares when we worry. Jesus says to cast the whole, not part, but ALL of your cares on Him. Give it all to God! When we hold on to our cares, Satan is there waiting. That's why we have to pay attention. Remember, Satan goes after those who are weak.

We are required to have faith in order to walk in Him.

*2 Corinthians 5:7 (KJV)*
*"For we walk by faith, not by sight."*

If we are listening and being attentive to Him, we will always know which direction to go. When we know our shepherd, He will steer us clear of all trouble.

*John 10:27-28 (KJV)*
*"My sheep hear my voice, and I know them, and they follow me: And I give unto them eternal life; and they shall never perish, neither shall any man pluck them out of my hand."*

As His sheep, we can train our ear to always listen to His voice. We understand that if He is saying, "My sheep are listening to my voice", that means there are other voices. Only by following His voice will we receive eternal life and never perish. We will live the full life He has for us. There is nobody and nothing in this world that can pluck us out of His hand!

We have a Shepherd who cares for us and we should cast all our cares upon Him.

**Mark 4:35-41 (KJV)**
*"And the same day, when the even was come, he saith unto them, Let us pass over unto the other side. And when they had sent away the multitude, they took him even as he was in the ship. And there were also with him other little ships. And there arose a great storm of wind, and the waves beat into the ship, so that it was now full. And he was in the hinder part of the ship, asleep on a pillow: and they awake him, and say unto him, Master, carest thou not that we perish?"*

Here we will examine each verse.

*Mark 4:35, "And the same day, when the even was come, he saith unto them, Let us pass over unto the other side."*

Jesus, our Chief Shepherd, says unto His disciples we are going to get in the boat and take it to the other side. As our good Shepherd, we all know Jesus and we can cast all of our cares on Him. Jesus cannot lie, so when He says to His disciples, "We are going to the other side." We know that He knew the boat would get to the other side!

> *Mark 4:36, "And when they had sent away the multitude, they took him even as he was in the ship. And there were also with him other little ships."*

Jesus and the disciples have left the shore and the ship is now headed for the other side.

> *Mark 4:37, "And there arose a great storm of wind, and the waves beat into the ship, so that it was now full."*

As they were headed to the other side, there was a great storm and the boat became full of water.

> *Mark 4:38, "And he was in the hinder part of the ship, asleep on a pillow: and they awake him, and say unto him, Master, carest thou not that we perish?"*

Jesus Christ, our Shepherd, has cast the whole of His care upon His Father, knowing that if His Father says, "We are going to the other side," we are going to the other side! He has this confidence in His heart. His disciples found that Jesus is sleeping during the trip and the storm.

We know in Jesus' time, that many people in that area were fishermen. Undoubtedly, many of Jesus' disciples were too; which meant that they have been in storms before. This scripture gives the impression that this storm had to be of abnormal size for the disciples to question their own faith (fate) and go to Jesus.

> *Mark 4:39, "And he arose, and rebuked the wind, and said unto the sea, Peace, be still. And the wind ceased, and there was a great calm."*

When He arose He was at peace, although the storm was all around Him. He said to the storm, "Be still." He had already told the disciples, "We are going to the other side," which meant they are going to the other side.

> *Mark 4:40, "And he said unto them, Why are ye so fearful? how is it that ye have no faith?"*

When He said to His disciples, "Why are you so fearful and how is it that you have no faith?" He was saying to them, "I expected your faith to do exactly what I just did. I expect you to have my same authority and for you to quiet the storm."

> *Mark 4:41, "And they feared exceedingly, and said one to another, What manner of man is this, that even the wind and the sea obey him?"*

The disciples became exceedingly fearful and said, "What manner of man is this, that even the wind and sea obey him?" Jesus was a man full of faith and He knew His Father was faithful. His disciples had no faith in this situation. How about in our own lives? How do we act or treat our situations? Just as He expected His disciples to have faith, He expects us to have faith. We have to know He cares and that He will supply all we need. God will supply all our needs according to His riches! You can't get any higher than that! Not your riches, it is according to God's riches. We must have the peace of God at all times. Satan is always trying to get into our thoughts. We have to remain in God's peace to calm the storms. There will be storms, but you and I should remain in the peace of Christ!

> *Proverbs 3:3 (AMP)*
> *"Let not mercy and kindness [shutting out all hatred and selfishness] and truth [shutting out all deliberate hypocrisy or falsehood] forsake you; bind them about your neck, write them upon the tablet of your heart."*

# Chapter 5:
# LIVING IN VICTORY

*Matthew 9:28-29 (KJV)*
*"And when he was come into the house, the blind men came to him: and Jesus saith unto them, Believe ye that I am able to do this? They said unto him, Yea, Lord. Then touched he their eyes, saying, According to your faith be it unto you."*

Jesus said to the blind man, "According to your faith be it unto you." I believe Jesus rose after His death and is now seated at the right hand of God.

*Hebrew 1:3 (KJV)*
*"Who being the brightness of his glory, and the express image of his person, and upholding all things by the word of his power, when he had by himself purged our sins, sat down on the right hand of the Majesty on high."*

"Who being in the brightness of His glory..." The glory is the nature of God revealed in its brightness! He is the expressed image of the Father. And whatever is in the Father, is revealed in the Son. He is unchangeable. He is full of love, life and power. He created and has sustained all things visible and invisible. He purged our sins. He sat down at the right hand of the Majesty on high.

Love, power and glory have been revealed to us by the Son of God!

*Galatians 5:6 (AMP)*
*"For [if we are] in Christ Jesus, neither circumcision nor uncircumcision counts for anything, but only faith activated and energized and expressed and working through love."*

God's plan is to purchase us through Christ. This plan consists of salvation, healing, and the fullness of the Spirit. In His plan, we are given the gifts of the Spirit and have the fruit of the Spirit. His plan gives us our authority and victory over the seen world, our flesh, the devil, and all the powers of darkness.

He poured out His love, but many of us haven't sought out what that really means. We have lived our lives through our own experiences of what we thought was love. We each were born from parents and have come to an understanding of what love is through their guidance, non-guidance, protection, non-protection, help, non-help, honesty, dishonesty, attention, neglect, teaching, non-teaching, and so many more characteristics to include, even murder. These characteristics have been followed by a feeling of being loved or being unloved. These feelings live on in every relationship and manifest in one way or another. There are the rich who have had their hearts torn by a love experience and through their bad experience of what they believed to be love they have taken their own life. They were guided by their experience! Our experiences are all a part of our carnal nature.

I have learned that if I am to maintain any kind of faith walk, I must put down my carnal nature. I have learned that the secret is letting the love of God work within my spirit.

*1 John 4:16 (KJV)*
*"And we have known and believed the love that God hath to us. God is love; and he that dwelleth in love dwelleth in God, and God in him."*

The carnal world gives us an unreal love. The reality of true love is only found in the reality of God. God's love far exceeds anything the false world pretends to give. The reality of God's love is-- God is love! Without God in us, we have no love and we can offer no love. We cannot be in love. Without the love of God, we cannot understand love, speak about love and can't write about love. He is the main ingredient! If I say 'I love you,' and God's not in me, I have knowingly or unknowingly given you a false representation of love. There is a saying that came from a song, "Nothing from nothing leaves nothing." That's true! In order for me to give you anything, I must first have it in my possession. It's the same thing with the Spirit of God. He must truly dwell in us. We must know and believe the love God has given to us. We must reside in Him. God is in us. With this truth, we can seek Him for more understanding of Him and of who He is, for God is Love.

*Matthew 6:33 (KJV)*
*"But seek ye first the kingdom of God, and his righteousness; and all these things shall be added unto you."*

According to the word, we are to seek first the kingdom of God. It doesn't say seek yourself first, your desires, your family, kids, job, money, friends or anything else. The word clearly says seek first the kingdom of God. He goes on to say and seek His righteousness. His righteousness is His conduct, His correctness and His same path., We are to seek Christ Jesus and seek to live in the faith of Jesus.

> *Galatians 2:19-20 ( KJV)*
> *"For I through the law am dead to the law, that I might live unto God. I am crucified with Christ: nevertheless I live; yet not I, but Christ liveth in me: and the life which I now live in the flesh I live by the faith of the Son of God, who loved me, and gave himself for me."*

Every day we must die to ourselves! In other words, the existence that we had without Christ in our life was a life of death. The life we had before Christ was the walking dead. We must die to the old thinking, and no longer live life by selfishness. We must recognize the Head of the Church, who is Christ the Chief Cornerstone. He was 100 percent man and 100 percent God, with 100 percent of God's love in Him, and He gave us 100 percent of God's love. When we die to ourself, He reigns. As we follow Him by Faith, we know He has given to us. He also has put Himself in us and we now live. It is not that we live of ourselves but it is the Christ that lives on in us.

> *Hebrews 12:1-3 (KJV)*
> *"Wherefore seeing we also are compassed about with so great a cloud of witnesses, let us lay aside every weight, and the sin which doth so easily beset us, and let us run with patience the race that is set before us, Looking unto Jesus the author and finisher of our faith; who for the joy that was set before him endured the cross, despising the shame, and is set down at the*

*right hand of the throne of God. For consider him that endured such contradiction of sinners against himself, lest ye be wearied and faint in your minds."*

He who is the same, yesterday, today and forever, will never fail. Child of God, fix your eyes upon Him, and you shall never fail if you know how to continue in the good fight of faith. Follow His steps, imitate His every action, and mold your life after His example. If we keep looking unto the author and finisher of our faith, we will never miss the mark of God's holy standard of righteousness.

God is the Author, the Farmer, the Architect of all things and He has a design for us. Our life should be designed to His specifications. It is our job to seek out His design. When we line up with Him, there is always success. He has given us His Spirit, as a plan blueprint, to be constructed or developed in our lives in the natural. If you line up with His word, then you are in faith.

As the farmer, you decide what is to be grown, where you are going to grow it, what you need in order for it to grow, and how you are going to grow it. The farmer never asks the seed, "Hey seed, where would you like to be planted?" The seed never says to the farmer, "Hey, I don't like where you are putting me. I want to be planted over there!" The farmer knows how his crops are to be planted and when the crop is planted on good soil, there is a harvest.

God, as our Farmer, has planted his harvest through His Son Jesus Christ and He is the good soil. We, as the harvest of Christ, must continue growing in the good soil. If He says to tithe, we tithe. If He says to go to church, we go to church. If He says to have a pastor, we have a pastor. When He gives a direction within His constructed plan; it is given to perfect us.

Many of us have questioned the loving guidance which God has given to lead us to happiness. Take tithing for instance. Many question the purpose of tithing, argue about the tithes, or just don't tithe. If we know God's love for us, we will tithe without question. He is our loving Father. Most people don't realize the multiple purposes of why God has placed tithing in our lives. Tithing is a way of teaching us that God must be our first priority. Think of it this way, God owns all the money in the world. Do we really think He needs the money we possess? No. God is far above anything, including the money you are holding on to. He is our prosperity and the source of our wealth. When He gives you His money, why do you think He is giving it to you? The money you are holding on to, should be used in bringing others to the body of Christ. You are holding on to it for your own personal reasons and wondering why you never have enough. You haven't given it to be a blessing to someone else. Because of your own selfishness and plan, you now have interfered with the blessing that God wanted to give back to you. His plan was a greater blessing.

> *Luke 6:38 (KJV)*
> *"Give, and it shall be given unto you; good measure, pressed down, and shaken together, and running over, shall men give into your bosom. For with the same measure that ye mete withal it shall be measured to you again."*

He says to give and it shall be given unto you. Do you trust and believe in His Word? We have to remember He is God. He is never changing. What He says, you can believe. When you don't trust and believe Him, you're not in faith and are not in line with

His word. The blessing that was for you will not work in your life because you chose not to remain in it. You became the seed that decided to do it their own way and not by the Farmer's design.

There is a design and a purpose in the will of God for every area of our lives. Seeking them out gives a strong indication of the quality of our faith, and will lead those who are persistent to victory in every area of their lives. We must continue to press toward the mark!

> *Philippians 3:13-14 (KJV)*
> *"Brethren, I count not myself to have apprehended: but this one thing I do, forgetting those things which are behind, and reaching forth unto those things which are before, I press toward the mark for the prize of the high calling of God in Christ Jesus."*

Every day should be a day of learning and growth with our Father. We should reach for God's spiritual understanding. In the morning, we should thank Him for who He is, thank Him for His Son Jesus Christ, thank Him for the Holy Spirit, and ask the Holy Spirit to guide us on our day. Let us continue to ask for more of His will, more of His power, more of His glory. Then let us pick up the word of God and let the word construct us into the design our Father has built for us. A building not made with hands, but one that eternally loves. We are to meditate on Him daily, all day long!

We will listen to the instruction given to us by the Holy Spirit! We will keep the book of the law upon our lips! Our body is the temple of God! Where He leads, we will follow. What we proclaim out of our mouth, is what the Father and the Son have spoken to us, through the Holy Spirit. Wherever we stand, the Kingdom of God is with us. We have all the power and all the glory within us because of Jesus. We have prosperity, and where prosperity is, there is balance. Everywhere we stand the kingdom of God will be there because of Jesus. The victory is in us, and upon us!

Realizing that our help comes from above, we must have a true belief in God and know He cares for us. We must continue believing with unwavering conviction, that our victory is instilled in us. We have a peace with God, that produces the peace of God! We have a real faith, that rises above head faith. Head faith only moves your mouth. Child of God-- real faith will influence our behavior. There shall be no temptation known to man that will overtake us. We know God is faithful in all things. Our inner man shall remain in the peace of Christ with a faith that moves mountains.

Now when we have that wrong thought, dream, experience or memory, we can cast it down in the name of Jesus. We are being dressed in faith because of our obedience to Christ. We have adapted, are adapting, and will continue to adapt to a new way of life, the life in Christ.

### *A PRAYER IN AGREEMENT WITH GOD:*

*Ephesian 3:14-19 (KJV)*
*"For this cause I bow my knees unto the Father of our Lord Jesus Christ, Of whom the whole family in heaven and earth is named, That he would grant you, according to the riches of his glory, to be strengthened with might by his Spirit in the inner man; That Christ may dwell in your hearts by faith; that ye, being*

*rooted and grounded in love, May be able to comprehend with all saints what is the breadth, and length, and depth, and height; And to know the love of Christ, which passeth knowledge, that ye might be filled with all the fulness of God."*

Christ is our victory! I will continue in His faith. I'm not leaving it to the Dogs! In Jesus name. Amen.

# Chapter 6:
# FAITH BUILDS – FRUIT OF THE SPIRIT SCRIPTURES

When we gave our lives to Jesus, He instilled Spiritual fruit in us. If we are walking in His faith, this fruit is revealed. Notice the order of the fruit of the Spirit. It begins with Love, without love, you can't have the fullness of the fruit.

*Galatians 5:22-23 (KJV)*
*"But the fruit of the Spirit is love, joy, peace, longsuffering, gentleness, goodness, faith, Meekness, temperance: against such there is no law."*

*Galatians 5:22 -23 (CEB)*
*"But the fruit of the Spirit is love, joy, peace, patience, kindness, goodness, faithfulness, gentleness, and self-control."*

**LOVE**

*1 John 4:8 (KJV)*
*"He that loveth not knoweth not God; for God is love."*

*1 Corinthians 13:4-6 (NIV)*
*"Love is patient, love is kind. It does not envy, it does not boast, it is not proud. It does not dishonor others, it is not self-seeking, it is not easily angered, it keeps no record of wrongs. Love does not delight in evil but rejoices with the truth."*

## JOY

*James 1:2 (KJV)*
*"My brethren, count it all joy when ye fall into divers temptations."*

## PEACE

*John 14:27 (KJV)*
*"Peace I leave with you; My peace I give to you; not as the world gives, do I give to you. Let not your heart be troubled, nor let it be fearful."*

*John 16:33 (KJV)*
*"These things I have spoken to you, that in Me you may have peace. In the world you have tribulation, but take courage; I have overcome the world."*

*Philippians 4:6-7 (KJV)*
*"Be anxious for nothing, but in everything by prayer and supplication with thanksgiving let your requests be made known to God. And the peace of God, which surpasses all comprehension, shall guard your hearts and your minds in Christ Jesus."*

## PATIENCE

*Luke 8:15 (KJV)*
*"But that on the good ground are they, which in an honest and good heart, having heard the word, keep it, and bring forth fruit with patience."*

## KINDNESS

*John 15:13 (KJV)*
*"Greater love has no one than this, that someone lay down his life for his friends."*

*Luke 6:35 (KJV)*
*"But love ye your enemies, and do good, and lend, hoping for nothing again; and your reward shall be great, and ye shall be the children of the Highest: for he is kind unto the unthankful and to the evil."*

*Proverbs 16:7 (KJV)*
*"When a man's ways please the LORD, he makes even his enemies to be at peace with him."*

*Ephesians 4:32 (KJV)*
*"And be ye kind one to another, tenderhearted, forgiving one another, even as God for Christ's sake hath forgiven you."*

## GOODNESS

*Romans 8:28 (KJV)*
*"And we know that for those who love God all things work together for good, for those who are called according to his purpose."*

## FAITHFULNESS

*1 Corinthians 1:9 (KJV)*
*"God is faithful, by whom ye were called unto the fellowship of his Son Jesus Christ our Lord."*

*Proverbs 3:3 (KJV)*
*"Let not mercy and truth forsake thee: bind them about thy neck; write them upon the table of thine heart."*

*Mark 11:22-24 (AMP)*
*"And Jesus, replying, said to them, Have faith in God [constantly]. Truly I tell you, whoever says to this mountain, Be lifted up and thrown into the sea! and does not doubt at all in his heart but believes that what he says will take place, it will be done for him. For this reason I am telling you, whatever you ask for in prayer, believe (trust and be confident) that it is granted to you, and you will [get it]."*

## GENTLENESS

*Matthew 11:29 (KJV)*

*"Take my yoke upon you, and learn of me; for I am meek and lowly in heart; and ye shall find rest unto your soul."*

*Galatians 5:25 (KJV)*
*"If we live in the Spirit, let us also walk in the Spirit."*

## SELF-CONTROL

*Proverbs 25:28 (KJV)*
*He that hath no rule over his own spirit is like a city that is broken down, and without walls.*

*2 Peter 1:3-8 (KJV)*
*"According as his divine power hath given unto us all things that pertain unto life and godliness, through the knowledge of him that hath called us to glory and virtue: Whereby are given unto us exceeding great and precious promises: that by these ye might be partakers of the divine nature, having escaped the corruption that is in the world through lust. And beside this, giving all diligence, add to your faith virtue; and to virtue knowledge; And to knowledge temperance; and to temperance patience; and to patience godliness; And to godliness brotherly kindness; and to brotherly kindness charity. For if these things be in you, and abound, they make you that ye shall neither be barren nor unfruitful in the knowledge of our Lord Jesus Christ."*

www.ingramcontent.com/pod-product-compliance
Lightning Source LLC
Chambersburg PA
CBHW071645040426
42452CB00009B/1768